STUDY GUIDE
Theodore Schultz

WESTERN CIVILIZATION

A Social and Cultural History

VOLUME II
1500 - The Present

MARGARET L. KING

Brooklyn College and the Graduate Center
City University of New York

Prentice Hall, Upper Saddle River, New Jersey 07458

©2000 by PRENTICE-HALL, INC.
PEARSON EDUCATION
Upper Saddle River, New Jersey 07458

All rights reserved

10 9 8 7 6 5 4 3 2 1

ISBN-0-13-014821-0

Printed in the United States of America

CONTENTS

Chapter 15: Absolute Power: War and Politics in Early Modern Europe 1500 - 1750	135
Chapter 16: Europe Reaches Out: Global Voyages and Cultural Encounters 1500 - 1750	147
Chapter 17: The Age of Reason: Science, Enlightenment, and Revolution 1500 - 1900	158
Chapter 18: Town, Court, and Country: Privilege and Poverty in Early Modern Europe 1500 - 1780	167
Chapter 19: Inalienable Rights: Revolution and its Promises in Anglo- and Latin America 1500 - 1880	175
Chapter 20: Revolt and Reorganization in Europe: From Absolute Monarchy to the Paris Commune 1750 - 1871	185
Chapter 21: Machines in the Garden: The Industrialization of the West 1750 - 1914	195
Chapter 22: Lives of the Other Half: Western Society in an Industrial Age 1750 - 1914	204
Chapter 23: The Western Imperium: European Migration, Settlement, and Domination around the Globe 1750 - 1914	213
Chapter 24: Storm, Stress, and Doubt: European Culture from Classicism to Modernism 1780 - 1914	223
Chapter 25: The Mighty are Fallen: The Trauma of World War I 1914 - 1920	233
Chapter 26: The Triumph of Uncertainty: Cultural Innovation, Social Disruption, and Economic Collapse 1915 - 1945	242
Chapter 27: States in Conflict: Communism, Fascism, Democracy, and the Crisis of World War II 1917 - 1945	252
Chapter 28: The End of Imperialism: Decolonization and Statebuilding around the Globe 1914 - 1990s	262
Chapter 29: Back from Armageddon: From the Bomb to the Internet	271
Chapter 30: Epilogue: The Last Decade: Where We've Been and What May Be: The 1990s	280

CHAPTER 15: ABSOLUTE POWER
WAR AND POLITICS IN EARLY MODERN EUROPE
1500 – 1750

OVERVIEW:

The splintering of the Christian Church and technological innovation result in the birth of the modern nation-state, where power is exercised by national governments. This competition between these governments, and the attempts by the Church to exert control, lead inexorably to war. Out of these wars and their excesses, a movement develops that governments are not absolute, but rather should be subject to the rights of citizens.

OUTLINE:

Prologue: The Perfect Prince

I. Power and Gunpowder
      A. Knights and Guns
      B. Military Organization

II. War Games
      A. Wars Over Faith and Turn, 1500 – 1648
      B. State in Competition, 1648 – 1763

III. An Age of Kings
      A. Spain: Religious Zeal and Royal Absolutism
      B. France: The Apogee of Absolutism
      C. England: The Sharing of Power
      D. Three New Empires: The Reshaping of Eastern Europe

III. Mirrors for Princes
      A. The Idea of the Prince
      B. Halls of Mirrors
      C. Roman Law and Natural Right

Conclusion: Power, Resistance, and the Meaning of the West

IDENTIFICATION:

Rasion d'etat

Courtiers

Infantry

Arquebus

Pike

Musket

Bayonet

Field of Golden Spurs

Cannon

Curtain Walls

Bastions

Musketeers

Cantons

Gustavus II Adolphus

Ambassador

Diplomacy

Prince William I

Fortress of Gibraltar

Asiento

The Three Estates

Absolutism

Mercantilism

Parlements

Intendance

The Sun King

Henry VIII

Elizabeth I

Mary Stuart

Parliament

Oliver Cromwell

Charles II

Restoration

Mary II

William III

Glorious Revolution

Phillip II

Ivan III

Ivan IV

Jean Bodin

Bishop Jacques Benigne Bossuet

True Law of Free Monarchy

Thomas Hobbes

"Monstrous Regiment of Women"

Androgyny

Catherine de'Medici

MULTIPLE CHOICE:

1. Raison d'etat means:
    a. reason of being
    b. reason of knowledge
    c. reason of state
    d. none of the above

2. The advent of guns clinched the triumph of:
    a. infantry over Cavalry
    b. cavalry over Infantry
    c. ships over cavalry
    d. none of the above

3. Bayonets made the pike:
    a. obsolete
    b. necessary
    c. useful
    d. none of the above

4. Which came first in Europe?
    a. the cannon
    b. the arquebus
    c. the musket
    d. the rifle

5. Michaelangelo designed:
    a. ships
    b. muskets
    c. fortifications
    d. cannon

6. The tends in international politics characteristics of the early modern era first emerged in:
    a. France
    b. Norway
    c. Spain
    d. Italy

7. Prince William I was nicknamed:
    a. the Pious
    b. the Silent
    c. the Terrible
    d. the Great

8. Suleiman I was nicknamed:
    a. the Magnificent
    b. the Silent
    c. the Pious
    d. the Great

9. Absolutism was not a part of which country?
    a. Spain
    b. France
    c. England
    d. none of the above

10. Which of the following would describe Charles II?
    a. sickly
    b. stupid
    c. impotent
    d. all of the above

11. Which of the following was not an estate of France?
    a. clergy
    b. nobility
    c. shipowners
    d. commoners

12. Louis XIV was known as the:
    a. the Sun King
    b. the Moon King
    c. the Great
    d. the Silent

13. Catherine de Medeci identified herself as which Greek God?
    a. Athena
    b. Zuez
    c. Artemis
    d. Saturn

14. Elizabeth I of England had how many consorts officially?
    a. three
    b. two
    c. one
    d. none

ESSAY:

1. The Europeans encountered gunfire for the first time in 1240; by 1600, the Europeans were the masters of this armament. Why was Europe such a breeding ground for innovations in battlefield technology?

2. Did the era from 1500 – 1700 in Europe expose some of the dangers of monarchy as a form of government? What were they? Given these dangers, why did monarchs continue to rule?

3. Does the fact that so many women occupied positions of power during this period suggest that in general women were not oppressed in Europe? Why or why not?

4. What was the impact of the Dutch rebellion against Spain? Did that rebellion signal the beginning of the end of the Spanish empire?

5. What did the development of the modern state system mean for the power of the Catholic Church? Why?

CHRONOLOGY:

Match the events listed below to the appropriate place.

```
1500          1550          1600          1650          1700          1750
/_____/_____/_____/_____/_____/_____
```

A. Expulsion of Jews from Spain
B. U.S. Constitution ratified
C. Hobbes' Leviathan
D. Peace of Westphalia
E. Defeat of Spanish Armada
F. Glorious Revolution

MAP EXERCISE:

Label the following areas (refer to the map on page 462):
1. Austrian Habsburg possessions, 1795
2. Prussian possessions, 1795
3. Danish possessions, 1795
4. Ottoman Empire
5. Kingdom of Naples
6. Papal States
7. Swiss Confederacy
8. Russia

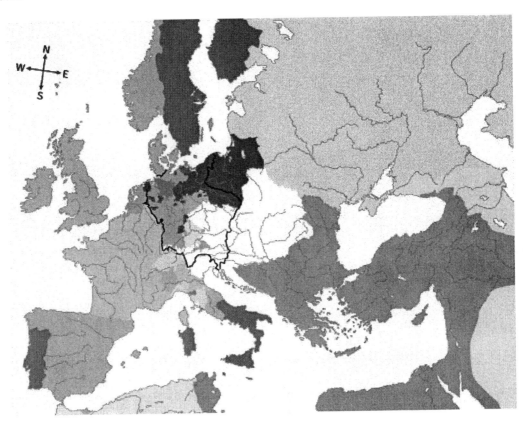

MULTIPLE CHOICE ANSWER KEY:

1. c, p. 450
2. a, p. 450
3. a, p. 451
4. a, p. 450
5. c, p. 451
6. d, p. 452
7. b, p. 456
8. a, p. 456
9. d, p. 463
10. d, p. 461
11. c, p. 461
12. a, p. 463
13. c, p. 472
14. d, p. 472

CHRONOLOGY ANSWER KEY:

Expulsion of Jews from Spain	1492
U.S. Constitution ratified	1788
Hobbes' Leviathan	1651
Peace of Westphalia	1648
Defeat of Spanish Armada	1588
Glorious Revolution	1688

CHAPTER 16: EUROPE REACHES OUT
GLOBAL VOYAGES AND CULTURAL ENCOUNTERS
1500 - 1750

OVERVIEW:

This chapter explores the rise of the European nation-states in a world governed by trade, exploration, and discovery. The changes wrought by these processes affected both the discoverers and those discovered, and set the foundation of the modern geopolitical world.

OUTLINE:

Prologue: Who is the Cannibal?

I. THE OPEN SEAS
    A. Portugal Takes the Lead
    B. Old World Ventures

II. BRAVE NEW WORLD
    A. Exploration and Conquest
    B. Patterns of Settlement
    C. Encountering Others
    D. The African Solution

III. THE WEALTH OF NATIONS
    A. Bringing Home the Bacon
    B. Trade Wars

Conclusion: The Expansion of Europe and the Meaning of the West.

IDENTIFICATION:

Ocean Sea

Sextant

Lateen

Samurai

Spice Islands

Portolan

Caravel

Conquistadors

Astrolabe

Meridians

African Route

Creole

Quadrant

Dhows

Joint Stock Companies

Plantation Systems

Laus of Burgos

Mestizos

Snuff

South Sea Bubble

New Laws

Mulattoes

Reales

Stock Exchanges

Microbe Shock

Abolition

Peso

Peace of Utrect

Indentured Servants

Species

Louisiana Bubble

Amsterdam

MULTIPLE CHOICE:

1. The compass was first used by _____ navigators.
    a. Arab
    b. European
    c. Chinese
    d. Amerindian

2. The astrolabe was invented by a _____ scientist.
    a. Arab
    b. Greek
    c. Chinese
    d. African

3. Prince Henry the Navigator was a ruler of _____.
    a. England
    b. France
    c. Spain
    d. Portugal

4. Vasco de Goma accomplished which of the following?
    a. he was the first European to sail around African to India.
    b. he was the first European to sail the Red Sea.
    c. he was the first European in America.
    d. he standardized Portuguese taxes.

5. The Muslin eunuch Zheng was an explorer for:
   a. Japan
   b. China
   c. France
   d. India

6. The _____ were the first Europeans to discover the Southern tip of South America.
   a. Vikings
   b. Spanish
   c. Portuguese
   d. Dutch

7. _____ was the first to circumnavigate the globe.
   a. Magellan
   b. Columbus
   c. Neon
   d. Vespuchi

8. Hernan Cortes destroyed the _____ empire.
   a. Incan
   b. Aztec
   c. Mayan
   d. Dutch

9. The Amerindian languages descended from a common pool of _____ languages.
   a. European
   b. African
   c. Asian
   d. Invented

10. The Americans obtained _____ from Europeans.
    a. gunpowder
    b. horses
    c. steel
    d. all of the above

11. Bartoleme de las Casas committed himself to which cause?
    a. Christianizing the Muslims
    b. converting the Amerindians
    c. stopping Spanish brutality
    d. stopping syphilis

12. Most slaves in the Middle Ages were from _____.
    a. Africa
    b. Asia or Slavic Europe
    c. Italy
    d. Britain

13. Arabs enslaved people of what color?
    a. black
    b. white
    c. any
    d. none: they did not practice slavery

14. The first North American slaves from Africa were transported by the:
    a. Dutch
    b. French
    c. Portuguese
    d. English

15. Large scale economic growth caused which problem in Europe in the 1700's?
    a. scurvy
    b. smallpox
    c. inflation
    d. plague

ESSAY:

1. Compare and contrast the enslavement of Africans with the enslavement of Amerindians.

2. Compare and contrast the exploratory policies of the Portuguese, Dutch and English.

3. Describe the slave trade from the view of an African. Who sold the slave into slavery? Who transported the slave? Who bought the slave?

4. Why did the Europeans treat Africans, Amerindians, Arabs, and Asians differently? For example: Why did the Europeans colonize the Americans, but not Africa? Why did the Europeans seek to economically dominate the Far East, but not Arabia?

5. Is the explorer a villain, a hero, both, or neither? Should we venerate explorers for their bravery, or condemn them for their destruction?

CHRONOLOGY:

Match the events listed below to the appropriate place.

```
1500            1550            1600            1650            1700
/_____/_____/_____/_____/
```

A. Thirty Years' War
B. Cortes conquers Mexico
C. Magellan sails the world
D. Luther's 95 Theses
E. De la Salle explores Mississippi Valley

MAP EXERCISE:

A. Label the colonial possession for each of the following countries (refer to the map on page 505):
1. Portugal
2. Spain
3. Holland
4. England
5. France

B. Draw the trade routes followed by the following explorers:
1. Arab
2. Chinese
3. English

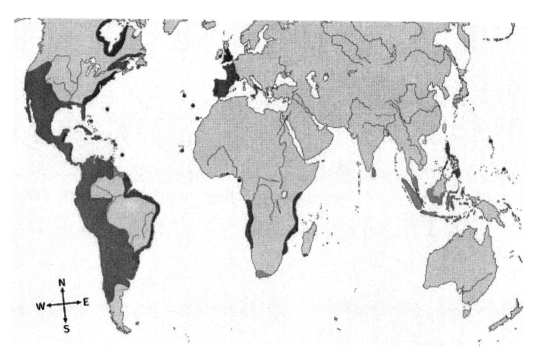

MULTIPLE CHOICE ANSWER KEY:

1. c, p. 481
2. b, p. 480
3. d, p. 482
4. a, p. 482
5. b, p. 485
6. b, p. 491
7. a, p. 491
8. b, p. 492
9. c, p. 496
10. d, p. 496
11. c, p. 498
12. b, p. 499
13. c, p. 499
14. c, p. 500
15. c, p. 508

CHRONOLOGY ANSWER KEY:

Thirty Years' War	1618-1648
Cortes conquers Mexico	1519-1521
Magellan sails the world	1519-1522
Luther's 95 Theses	1517
De la Salle explores Mississippi Valley	1682

CHAPTER 17: THE AGE OF REASON
SCIENCE, ENLIGHTENMENT, AND REVOLUTION
1500 - 1900

OVERVIEW:

A revolution in thought focusing on the human as opposed to the divine freed western thinkers from the dogma of the past, but also freed them from the past's moral guidance. Thus, the era of the Enlightenment opened the West to an age of new discovery, but also set the stage for incredible cultural upheaval.

OUTLINE:

Prologue: Descartes' Dilemma

I. New Heaven, New Earth: The Scientific Revolution
    A. The Advent of Infinity
    B. "Man the Machine": Exploration of the Human Body
    C. Hard Facts and Pure Reason: New Modes of Thinking
    D. The End of Magic

II. The Lights Go On: The Enlightenment
    A. Common Sense
    B. Social Contracts
    C. Other Places, Other Customs

III. The Little Learning: Literacy and Education
    A. Pleasure Reading
    B. A Cat and a Catte: Women and Learning
    C. Halls of Reason: The Social Context

IV. Conclusion: Descartes' Dilemma and the Meaning of the West

IDENTIFICATION:

Descartes

Rationalism

Copernicus

Brahe

Kepler

Bruno

Galileo

Newton

Humors

Alchemy

Skepticism

Deductive

Empirical

Hypothesis

Astrology

Cartography

Enlightenment

Paine

Voltaire

Deism

Les Salons

MULTIPLE CHOICE:

1. Copernicus published his view of a sun-centered universe
    a. on his death bed
    b. in his third year at the University
    c. as a challenge to the Pope
    d. none of the above

2. Brahe's main contribution to astronomy was:
    a. the training of astronomers
    b. the discovery of a new comet
    c. his meticulous observations
    d. the construction of a telescope

3. Kepler demonstrated which of the following:
    a. the planets move in circles around the sun
    b. the planets move in intersecting orbits
    c. the planets move in ellipses
    d. the planets all move at the same speed

4. Bruno was burned at the stake for:
   a. adultery
   b. rebellion against the Pope
   c. pursuit of black magic
   d. pantheism

5. Galileo wrote about his discoveries in:
   a. Latin
   b. Italian
   c. Greek
   d. English

6. Newton defined the principle of universal:
   a. gravitation
   b. motion
   c. time
   d. energy

7. Lady Mary Wortley Montagu is credited with bringing to Europe a cure for which disease?
   a. Cholera
   b. Plague
   c. Typhoid
   d. Smallpox

8. Astrology was an accepted science until which century?
   a. the fifteenth
   b. the sixteenth
   c. the seventeenth
   d. the eighteenth

9. The most important *philosophe* was:
   a. Diderot
   b. Bayle
   c. Paine
   d. Voltaire

10. Deists believed that:
    a. there is no God.
    b. there is a God who permits the universe to operate according to natural law.
    c. there may be a God but you cannot prove it.
    d. the world is ruled by many Gods.

ESSAY:

1. What do you think the effect was in the rise in pleasure reading on European culture?

2. Is the enlightenment really related to a broad change in technology in culture, or does it really stem from the introduction of the printing press to Europe?

3. How would the idea that there is no difference between the minds of men and the minds of women be received in the twenty first century? Do you agree with that Enlightenment assertion?

4. Did the Enlightenment destroy European religion?

5. Was the Enlightenment merely the intellectual justification of Europe's increasing influence in the world? Do you think Europe saw its task to bring the Enlightenment to other parts of the world?

CHRONOLOGY:

Match the events listed below to the appropriate place.

1450   1500   1550   1600   1650   1700   1750   1800
/_____/_____/_____/_____/_____/_____/_____/_

A. Kant's "What is Enlightenment"
B. Locke's "Two Treatises of Government"
C. Galileo condemned
D. Martyr's "Chronicles of the New World"

MAP EXERCISE:

Label the dominant areas of the following religions (refer to map on page 524):
1. Protestant
2. Roman Catholic
3. Strong Protestant minorities within Roman Catholic areas
4. Eastern Orthodox

Locate and label the birthplace of each of the following Enlightenment thinkers:
1. Galileo
2. Montesquieu
3. Newton
4. Rousseau
5. Voltaire
6. Condorcet

MULTIPLE CHOICE ANSWER KEY:

1. a, p. 516
2. c, p. 517
3. c, p. 517
4. d, p. 517
5. b, p. 519
6. a, p. 519-20
7. d, p. 523
8. c, p. 527
9. d, p. 529
10. b, p. 531

CHRONOLOGY ANSWER KEY:

Kant's "What is Enlightenment" 1784
Locke's "Two Treatises of Government" 1690
Galileo condemned 1633
Martyr's "Chronicles of the New World" 1530

CHAPTER 18: TOWN, COURT, AND COUNTRY
PRIVILEGE AND POVERTY IN EARLY MODERN EUROPE
1500 - 1780

OVERVIEW:

This chapter explores the social and political culture of the west from 1500-1780. The gulf between rich and poor broadened, leading to an increased desire on the part of the poor to better themselves.

OUTLINE:

Prologue: The Would-Be Gentleman

I. Honorable Pursuits: The European Nobility of the Early Modern Age
    A. Lines and Houses
    B. Patterns of Nobility
    C. Courtiers and Kings

II. New Ways with New Wealth: The Early Modern Bourgeoisie
    A. The Ranks of the Bourgeoisie
    B. At Home
    C. Downtown
    D. Workers and Strangers

III. Field and Village: The Boundaries of Peasant Life
    A. Bread, Deans and Flocks
    B. Varieties of Labor
    C. Festival and Riot

Conclusion: The Privileged, The Poor, and the Meaning of the West

IDENTIFICATION:

Absolute Monarchy

Lines

Houses

Honor

Peer

Serf

Habsburg

Hidalgos

Bourgeoisie

Robot

MULTIPLE CHOICE:

1. Men and women were expected to show the nobility deference by:
    a. bowing or curtseying
    b. making way for them in the street
    c. yielding them the front pew in church
    d. all of the above

2. Which of the following arose first into the ranks of nobility?
    a. Nobles of the Robe
    b. Nobles of the Sword
    c. Nobles of the Marque
    d. Nobles of the Church

3. Commerce was considered _____ for noblemen.
    a. legal
    b. legal and honorable
    c. dishonorable
    d. dishonorable and sometimes illegal

4. The Nobles of Prussia were called:
    a. Hidalgos
    b. Junker
    c. The Liberum
    d. none of the above

5. The 1648 Insurrection in France was known as the:
    a. Hidalgos
    b. Habsburg
    c. Frond
    d. none of the above

6. Even during the Enlightenment, monarchs relied on nobles to:
    a. recruit armies
    b. keep order
    c. deal out justice
    d. none of the above

7. In the eighteenth century, women's dress became:
    a. less elaborate than men
    b. more elaborate than men
    c. as elaborate as men
    d. none of the above

8. By 1771 Benjamin Franklin had stood before how many kings:
    a. three
    b. four
    c. five
    d. six

9. Russian nobles in the 1700s measured their wealth by:
    a. acres of land
    b. numbers of serfs
    c. pounds of gold
    d. numbers of ships

10. In Catholic Europe the first estate referred to the:
    a. peasants
    b. townfolks
    c. nobles
    d. clergy

11. The last outbreak of plague in Europe was in:
    a. 1620
    b. 1720
    c. 1820
    d. 1920

12. The gallows in Europe during the Enlightenment was located:
    a. by the Courthouse
    b. by the Church
    c. by the gate to the City
    d. none of the above

13. Women's lives in the early modern period revolved around their:
    a. sexuality
    b. economic ability
    c. status at birth
    d. wealth

14. Until just a century ago, which of the following was the greatest cause of improved health for most Europeans?
    a. new medicines
    b. an understanding of surgical technique
    c. more food
    d. cleaner water

ESSAY:

1. To what extent was the creation of the Nobility of the Robe a reflection of the changing conditions of Europe from 1500 to 1780?

2. In your opinion, was the age of Enlightenment more or less violent than the high Middle Ages?

3. For what reason were nobles disinclined to engage in commerce?

4. How did the Enlightenment change the role of women compared to their role in the Middle Ages? Did these changes apply everywhere or only to women in certain ranges?

5. Did the continued existence of pre-Christian pagan practices suggest that the Enlightenment did not change much in European culture?

CHRONOLOGY:

Match the events listed below to the appropriate place

1450   1500   1550   1600   1650   1700   1750   1800
/_____/_____/_____/_____/_____/_____/_____/_

A. The Fronde
B. 10% Europeans live in cities
C. Final Partition of Poland
D. Russian Table of Ranks
E. Last major outbreak of Plague

MAP EXERCISE:

Label the following areas with the correct degree of peasant emancipation up to the year 1812 (refer to the map on page 569).
1. full emancipation
2. completely freed during the French Revolution (1789-1815)
3. peasants achieving personal freedom during Napoleonic era (1799-1815)
4. in process of achieving freedom
5. peasants remaining unfree

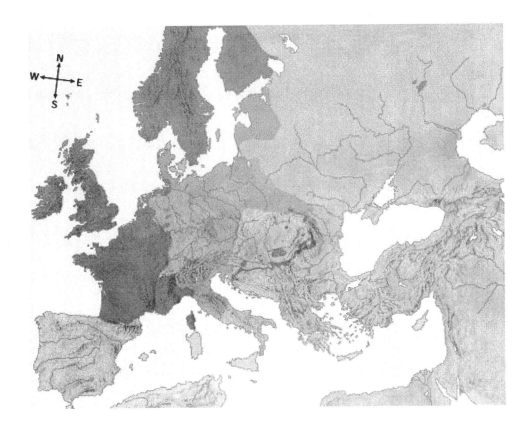

MULTIPLE CHOICE ANSWER KEY:

1. d, p. 548
2. b, p. 548
3. d, p. 548
4. b, p. 550
5. c, p. 551
6. d, p. 552-53
7. b, p. 553-54
8. c, p. 556
9. b, p. 569
10. d, p. 557
11. d, p. 565
12. b, p. 565
13. d, p. 564
14. b, p. 565

CHRONOLOGY ANSWER KEY:

The Fronde	1648-53
10% Europeans live in cities	1600
Final Partition of Poland	1795
Russian Table of Ranks	1722
Last major outbreak of Plague	1720

CHAPTER 19: INALIENABLE RIGHTS
REVOLUTION AND ITS PROMISES IN ANGLO-AND
LATIN AMERICA 1500 – 1880

OVERVIEW:

The encounter between the Old World and New the fruits of the Enlightenment, and the failure of the rich to share power with the poor all lead to revolution and rebellion. Ultimately, these revolutions demonstrated the New-World idea that stable societies share political power among the majority of their members.

OUTLINE:

Prologue: Jefferson's Promise

I. Old and New in the New World
    A. Brazil and the Caribbean: Plantation and Nations
    B. Spanish America: Mine, *Hacienda*, and Village
    C. The North Atlantic Coast: The Beckoning Wilderness

II. Declarations of Independence
    A. Atlantic North America: War for Independence
    B. Revolution in Haiti and Mexico
    C. Transition in Brazil and Paraguay
    D. Spanish South America: Victory at Ayacucho

III. Fulfilling the Promise
    A. The Reign of the *Caudillo*
    B. By the People

Conclusion: Jefferson's Promise, Lincoln's Pledge and the Meaning of the West

IDENTIFICATION:

Caribs

Arawaks

Voodoo

Mulattoes

Peninsulares

Mercantilism

Casa de Contratacion

Hacienda

Encomiendas

Peons

Castas

Viceroyalty

Audiencias

Creole

Primogeniture

Yeoman Farmer

Established Religion

Declaration of Independence

Loyalists

Federal Articles of Confederation

Bill of Rights

Francois Dominique Toussaint L'Ouverture

Miguel Hidalgo

Caudillo

Diego Rivera

Porfirio Diaz

Positivism

Pueblo

Elizabeth Stanton

Susan B. Anthony

Frederick Douglas

Abolitionism

Suffrage

Naturalized

MULTIPLE CHOICE:

1. Which of the following were Caribbean Amerindians?
    a. Mohawks
    b. Tainos
    c. Tome
    d. None of the above

2. Which of the following encouraged initial development of Rio de Janeiro?
    a. gold
    b. silver
    c. copper
    d. tin

3. Peninsulares were people from:
   a. Portugal
   b. Brazil
   c. France
   d. Italy

4. In 1670, the largest city in the New World was:
   a. New Amsterdam
   b. New Orleans
   c. Potosi
   d. San Juan

5. Spanish colonial rule was on the whole:
   a. inefficient
   b. efficient
   c. liberal
   d. conservative

6. The first resource exploited by Europeans in North America was:
   a. fish
   b. lumber
   c. gold
   d. silver

7. Attempt to impress Amerindians into labor were:
   a. successful
   b. efficient
   c. late
   d. futile

8. The established religion of British America was
   a. catholic
   b. protestant
   c. orthodox
   d. None of the above

9. The leaders of the colonial revolt against Parliament were:
   a. poor
   b. religious dissidents
   c. wealthy
   d. nobles

10. What percentage of colonists opposed the American Revolution:
    a. 10%
    b. 20%
    c. 30%
    d. 40%

11. Mexico obtained its freedom from Spain in what year?
    a. 1731
    b. 1831
    c. 1812
    d. 1915

12. South America freed itself from Spanish rule by when?
    a. 1810
    b. 1814
    c. 1820
    d. 1824

13. The Monroe Doctrine prevented:
    a. revolution
    b. rebellion
    c. recolonization
    d. none of the above

14. Benito Juarez was an:
    a. Amerindian
    b. Creole
    c. Negro
    d. none of the above

ESSAY:

1. How did slavery compare with serfdom described in the previous chapter? Which system was worse?

2. Describe the relationship between the abolitionist movement and the suffragist movement?

3. Why was it "enlightened" for the British Colonies to fight for self-rule in 1776, yet "unenlightened" for the Confederacy to seek self-rule in 1860?

4. Does the Dred Scott decision illuminate the limits of law in the West? Why or why not?

5. How did racial relations in Latin America differ from those in North America?

CHRONOLOGY:

Match the events listed below to the appropriate place.

```
1600      1650      1700      1750      1800      1850      1900
/_____/_____/_____/_____/_____/_____/_____
```

A. Seneca Falls Convention
B. Wounded Knee Massacre
C. Declaration of Independence
D. Dred Scott decision
F. Population of Buenos Aires, 250,000

MAP EXERCISE:

Label the approximate location of the following Indian tribes (refer to map on page 600):
1. Chippewa
2. Sioux
3. Comanche
4. Apache
5. Cheyenne
6. Pueblo

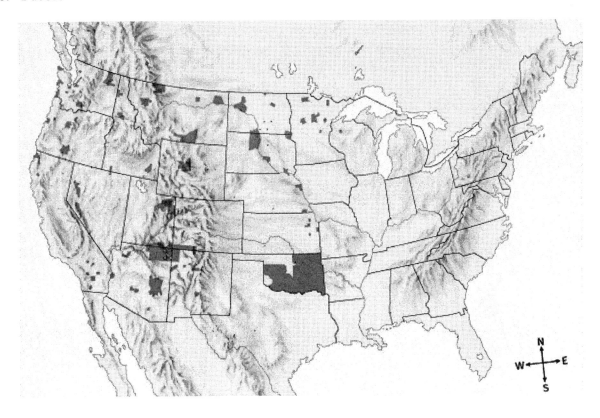

MULTIPLE CHOICE ANSWER KEY:

1. b, p. 576
2. a, p. 577
3. a, p. 578
4. c, p. 579
5. b, p. 581
6. a, p. 582
7. a, p. 583
8. d, p. 587
9. c, p. 589
10. b, p. 590
11. b, p. 591
12. d, p. 593
13. c, p. 593
14. a, p. 597

CHRONOLOGY ANSWER KEY:

Seneca Falls Convention	1848
Wounded Knee Massacre	1890
Declaration of Independence	1776
Dred Scott decision	1857
Population of Buenos Aires, 250,000	1869

CHAPTER 20: REVOLT AND REORGANIZATION IN EUROPE FROM ABSOLUTE MONARCHY TO THE PARIS COMMUNE 1750 – 1871

OVERVIEW:

In the Old World, the failure of the rich to share power broadly leads also to violent revolution – first in France, and then throughout the continent. Out of this bloodshed comes a consensus the rule of law, not the rule of kings, should be paramount.

OUTLINE:

Prologue: Thermidor

I. Preludes to Revolution
    A. Resistance to Absolutism
    B. Peasant Revolts and Free Trade
    C. The War of Ideas

II. The Rights of Man
    A. The Work of the National Assembly
    B. The Legislative Assembly and national Convention

III. The Birth of a Nation
    A. Peasants and Sans-Culottes
    B. The Culture of Revolution
    C. Reaction Sets In: The Directory

IV. The Imperial Adventure
    A. The Coming of Napoleon
    B. Napoleon's France
    C. Napoleon and the *Grande Armee*
    D. The Conservative Response

V. Power to the People
    A. Revolution and Counter-Revolution 1815-48
    B. Toward Accommodation: 1848-1871

Conclusion: Revolution, Counter-Revolution, and the Meaning of the West

IDENTIFICATION:

Thermidor

The Terror

Ancient Regime

Physiocrats

The Estates

The National Assembly

Jacobins

Robespierre

Girondins

Mary Wollstonecraft

Edmund Burke

Sans-Culottes

Committee of Public Safety

The Revolution

The Terror

Festival of the Supreme Being

Directory

Napoleon

Liberalism

Coup d'etat

Napoleonic Code

The Continental System

Waterloo

Nationalism

Conservatism

The Corn Laws

The Poor Law of 1834

The Great Hunger

The Second French Republic

The June Days

The Paris Commune

Dumas

MULTIPLE CHOICE:

1. Freemasonry was a(n):
    a. alternative to religion
    b. guild movement
    c. union
    d. none of the above

2. Physiocrats were:
    a. medical doctors
    b. religious writers
    c. Economic theorists
    d. none of the above

3. Robespierre led the:
    a. Girondins
    b. Jacobins
    c. Third Estate
    d. Order of Nobles

4. How many dissidents were imprisoned during The Terror?
    a. 300
    b. 3000
    c. 30,000
    d. 300,000

5. Robespierre argued that The Terror was:
    a. just
    b. unnecessarily brutal
    c. not part of the Revolution
    d. none of the above

6. Napoleon became First Consul in:
    a. 1801
    b. 1802
    c. 1803
    d. 1804

7. Napoleon became Emperor in:
    a. 1801
    b. 1802
    c. 1803
    d. 1804

8. Napoleon's France was ruled by what law?
    a. The Code
    b. Primogeniture
    c. Canon
    d. Common

9. Napoleon's battle tactics:
    a. had high casualties
    b. were innovative
    c. used columns
    d. all of the above

10. Russia employed which tactic against Napoleon?
    a. Hostage-taking
    b. Counter-insurgency
    c. Scorched-earth
    d. none of the above

11. The Congress of Vienna advocated
    a. Democracy
    b. revolution
    c. slavery
    d. conservatism

12. The plans of the congress of Vienna worked for _____ years:
    a. 5
    b. 10
    c. 15
    d. 20

13. There were _____ outbreaks of revolt in 1848 Europe.
    a. 5
    b. 20
    c. 50
    d. 100

14. The Parisian casualties in 1871 numbered:
    a. 5000
    b. 20,000
    c. 50,000
    d. 100,000

ESSAY:

1. Would the French Revolution have happened "but for" the French fiscal crisis of 1787?

2. What was the cause of the Terror? What was its ultimate effect?

3. What was Napoleon's greatest achievement? What was his greatest failure?

4. What was the effect of the French Revolution on women? Workers? Slaves?

5. What was the Paris Commune? Why did it fail?

CHRONOLOGY:

Match the events listed below to the appropriate place>

```
1750        1775        1800        1825        1850        1875        1900
/_____/_____/_____/_____/_____/_____/_____
```

A. Paris commune
B. "Year of Revolutions"
C. Waterloo
D. Fall of Robespierre
E. Tennis Court Oath

MAP EXERCISE:

Label the approximate area of the following battles during the French Revolution with either a "V" for a French victory, or a "D" for a French defeat (refer to map on page 620):
1. Hondshooste
2. Neerwinden
3. Valmy
4. Wattignies
5. Fleurus
6. Jemappes

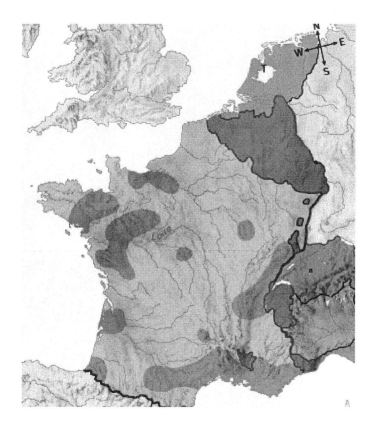

MULTIPLE CHOICE ANSWER KEY:

1. a, p. 611
2. a, p. 611
3. b, p. 615
4. d, p. 617
5. a, p. 617
6. b, p. 623
7. a, p. 624
8. a, p. 624
9. d, p. 625
10. c, p. 628
11. d, p. 628
12. c, p. 628
13. c, p. 633
14. b, p. 639

CHRONOLOGY ANSWER KEY:

Paris commune	1870
"Year of Revolutions"	1848
Waterloo	1815
Fall of Robespierre	1794
Tennis Court Oath	1789

CHAPTER 21: MACHINES IN THE GARDEN
THE INDUSTRIALIZATION OF THE WEST
1750 – 1914

OVERVIEW:

This chapter discusses the technological revolution that began in Britain and spread throughout the world from 1750 to 1914. The new industrialization made for a new world, but also led to wide-scale disruption in traditional society.

OUTLINE:

Prologue: Satanic Mills

I. Before Industrialization
    A. Medieval Foundations: The Urban Grid
    B. Early Modern Changes

II. Britain Industrializes
    A. Cotton and Water
    B. Coal and Water
    C. Iron, Coal, and Stream
    D. Railroad and Steamship

III. Catching Up
    A. The First Imitators
    B. The Rest of the West and the Asian
    C. Postponed Industrialization

Conclusion: Despoiled Gardens and the Meaning of the West

IDENTIFICATION:

Industrialization

Charters

Infrastructure

Putting Out System

Proto-industrial

Fallow

Enclosure

The Spinning Jenny

Pig Iron

Puddler

The Railroad

The Steam Ship

Zollverein

Cartells

Thomas Edison

Alexander Graham Bell

Gugliemo Marconi

Latifundias

MULTIPLE CHOICE:

1. _____ production spurred the miracle of British Industrialization
    a. Steel
    b. Income
    c. Cloth
    d. Gold

2. British industrialization led to Indian _____.
    a. slavery
    b. industrialization
    c. deindustrialization
    d. none of the above

3. British industrialization led to _____ work for American slaves.
    a. more
    b. less
    c. the same amount of
    d. None of the above

4. The first steam engine was patented in _____?
    a. 1598
    b. 1648
    c. 1698
    d. 1712

5. The creation of the steam engine had its greatest impact in what industry?
    a. textiles
    b. ceramics
    c. iron
    d. mining

6. Prior to 1800, steel was considered a:
    a. luxury
    b. necessity
    c. impossibility
    d. import

7. The _____ developed in tandem with the locomotive.
    a. airplane
    b. balloon
    c. steamship
    d. automobile

8. The chief rival of Britain in industrial output in 1873 was:
    a. Germany
    b. France
    c. Belgium
    d. The United States

9. The incandescent light bulb was invented by a(n):
    a. German
    b. Frenchman
    c. Englishman
    d. American

10. The leading exporter in 1913 was:
    a. Germany
    b. Britain
    c. France
    d. The United States

11. The only far-eastern country to industrialize before 1900 was:
    a. Korea
    b. China
    c. Japan
    d. Taiwan

12. Which of the following failed to industrialize by 1900?
    a. Latin America
    b. The Ottoman Empire
    c. India
    d. All of the above

13. Industrialization caused Enlightenment optimism to:
    a. increase
    b. disappear
    c. cloud over
    d. none of the above

ESSAY:

1. Of the nations that industrialized, which one changed the most? The least?

2. Which invention had the greatest immediate impact in the West: the steamship, the railroad, or the power loom. Why?

3. Why did some countries "de-industrialize" during the Industrial Revolution?

4. How did the "putting out" system impact industrialization in Britain?

5. Why were German industrial projects on a larger scale than those in Britain and France?

CHRONOLOGY:

Match the events listed below to the appropriate place.

1700   1725   1750   1775   1800   1825   1875   1900   1925
/_____/_____/_____/_____/_____/_____/_____/_____/

A. Cotton Gin
B. James Watt's Steam Engine
C. Transatlantic Cable Laid
D. The Great Exhibition
C. Lightbulb invented

MAP EXERCISE:

Locate and label the following major industrial towns (refer to map on page 666):
1. Belfast
2. Manchester
3. Danzig
4. St. Petersburg
5. Dresden
6. Lyons
7. Barcelona
8. Vienna

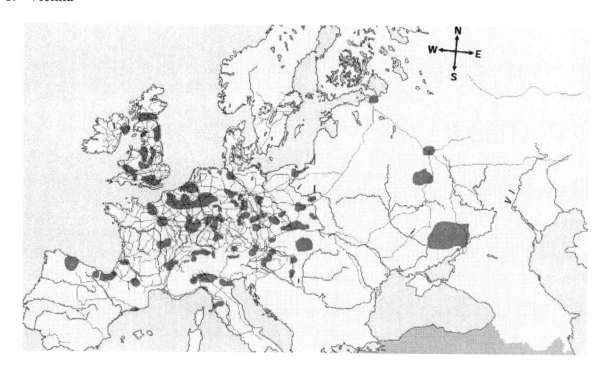

MULTIPLE CHOICE ANSWER KEY:

1. c, p. 647
2. c, p. 651
3. a, p. 651
4. c, p. 652
5. c, p. 654
6. a, p. 656
7. c, p. 656
8. a, p. 664
9. d, p. 669
10. d, p. 667
11. c, p. 670
12. d, p. 670
13. c, p. 672

CHRONOLOGY ANSWER KEY:

Cotton Gin	1793
James Watt's Steam Engine	1769
Transatlantic Cable Laid	1866
The Great Exhibition	1851
Lightbulb invented	1879

CHAPTER 22: LIVES OF THE OTHER HALF
WESTERN SOCIETY IN AN INDUSTRIAL AGE
1750 – 1914

OVERVIEW:

The rise of industrialization shifted the distribution of wealth in the West, but made the disparity between rich and poor even greater. In an effort to combat their oppressed status, workers banded together, leading to greater social unrest.

OUTLINE:

Prologue: Domains of Rich and Poor

I. Workers and Workplace
    A. Mine, Mill, and Factory
    B. The Birth of Labor

II. The Industrial City
    A. Boom Towns
    B. Structure and Infrastructure

III. The Two Halves at Home
    A. In the Tenement
    B. In the Townhouse

Conclusion: The One Half, the Other Half, and the Meaning of the West

IDENTIFICATION:

Artisans

Factory

Proletarian

Child Labor

Free Market

Trade Unions

Strike

Luddites

Communist

Utopia

Social Democratic

Collective Bargaining

Alien Nation

Demographic Tenement

Cholera

Courtesans

Slums Philanthropic Organizations

Sweated Industries

Music Hall

Antisepsis

MULTIPLE CHOICE:

1. Proletarians were:
    a. factory owners
    b. factory workers
    c. clergy
    d. politicians

2. Child labor was repudiated in what century?
    a. 15th
    b. 17th
    c. 19th
    d. 20th

3. The Luddites expressed dissatisfaction with working conditions by:
    a. strikes
    b. collective bargaining
    c. smashing machines
    d. all of the above

4. The populations of London in 1850 was approximately:
    a. 2,000,000
    b. 4,000,000
    c. 6,000,000
    d. 8,000,000

5. The London underground Rail Road opened in:
   a. 1853
   b. 1863
   c. 1903
   d. 1910

6. Industrialization led to an increase in demand for which kind of alcoholic beverage?
   a. beer
   b. wine
   c. distilled liquor
   d. mead

7. Prostitution _____ in the era of industrialization:
   a. flourished
   b. waned
   c. was unregulated
   d. none of the above

8. Rural households were more _____ than urban households.
   a. affluent
   b. liberal
   c. stable
   d. spacious

9. Sweated industry generally referred to:
   a. steel
   b. construction
   c. clothing
   d. shipbuilding

10. Anesthesia was originally in the form of:
    a. chloroform
    b. antisepsis
    c. tablets
    d. pills

11. In Britain, real wages between 1850 and 1875 increased by:
    a. one-quarter
    b. one-third
    c. one-half
    d. one-sixth

12. The majority of women in London and France at about 1900 were:
    a. industrial workers
    b. employers
    c. servants
    d. clerks

13. French syndicalists advocated coordinated strikes against:
    a. factories
    b. the state
    c. the church
    d. none of the above

14. Russian anarchists advocated:
    a. destruction of the factories
    b. destruction of the state
    c. destruction of the peasantry
    d. none of the above

ESSAY:

1. Was the average worker or artisan happier before or after the Industrial Revolution?

2. How were the lives of poor women after the Industrial Revolution? And their children?

3. How did technology change the urban landscape?

4. Who were the Luddites? Why were their tactics not successful?

5. In what nation were workers best treated in 1890? Why?

CHRONOLOGY:

Match the events listed below to the appropriate place

1750   1775   1800   1825   1850   1875   1900   1925
/_____/_____/_____/_____/_____/_____/_____/

A. Communist Manifesto
B. Paris Metro
C. New York Subway
D. Severe Cholera Epidemics London & Paris
E. Luddites Strike

MAP EXERCISE:

Locate and label the following cities with a population of over 1 million (refer to map on page 675):
1. Paris
2. London
3. Vienna
4. Berlin
5. St. Petersburg

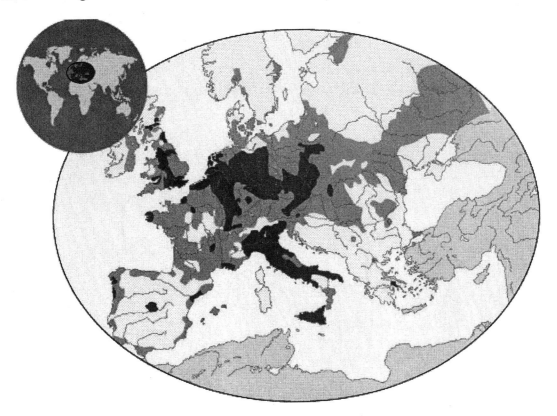

MULTIPLE CHOICE ANSWER KEY:

1. b, p. 676
2. d, p. 678
3. c, p. 676
4. a, p. 687
5. b, p. 690
6. c, p. 692
7. a, p. 692
8. c, p. 694
9. c, p. 695
10. a, p. 701
11. b, p. 697
12. c, p. 696
13. b, p. 684
14. b, p. 684

CHRONOLOGY ANSWER KEY:

Communist Manifesto	1848
Paris Metro	1900
New York Subway	1904
Severe Cholera Epidemics: London & Paris	1832
Luddites Strike	1811-1812

CHAPTER 23: THE WESTERN IMPERIUM EUROPEAN, MIGRATION, SETTLEMENT, AND DOMINATION AROUND THE GLOBE 1750 – 1914

OVERVIEW:

From 1500 to 1914, Western Culture slowly achieved dominance throughout the world because of the technological and social transformations discussed previously. This conquest was not without casualties – leading to a painful reckoning throughout the 20th Century.

OUTLINE:

Prologue: The Better Bookshelf

I. Lands of European Settlement: Colonial Ventures
    A. The Anglo-American Pattern
    B. The Spanish-American Pattern
    C. Autralasia: Another Anglophone Success
    D. The Russian Empire

II. Old World Encounters: Imperialism in Asia
    A. India: A Sub-continent Subdued
    B. The Philippines and East Indies
    C. China, Korea, and Indochina: Forced Entry
    D. Japan: Point, Counterpoint

III. Old World Encounters: Imperialism in the Middle East and Africa
    A. The Middle East: The Last Islamic Empire
    B. Sub-Saharan Africa: Divided and Despoiled

IV. Dominion Within
    A. The Irish: Despised and Persecuted
    B. The Jews: The Intimate Enemy
    C. The Psychology of Domination

V. Migrants and Money
    A. The Global System: Money and Goods
    B. The Global System: Peoples and Culture

Conclusion: The Western *Imperium* and the Meaning of the West

IDENTIFICATION:

Imperialism

Colonialism

Neocolonialism

Aborigines

Sepoys

Extraterritoriality

Concessions

Economic Imperialism

Quadi

Jihad

Mahdi

Theocracy

Quinine

Animist

Irish Question

The Kabbalah

Hasidism

Assimilation

Pogroms

Race

Ellis Island

MULTIPLE CHOICE:

1. The process of European expansion and domination of remote peoples is:
    a. imperialism
    b. colonialism
    c. neo-colonialism
    d. none of the above

2. The process of Europeans establishing settlements in largely undeveloped areas is:
    a. imperialism
    b. colonialism
    c. neo-colonialism
    d. none of the above

3. The economic policies of wealthy nations are often referred to as:
    a. imperialism
    b. colonialism
    c. neo-colonialism
    d. none of the above

4. The Russian Empire extended from Europe to:
    a. the Urals
    b. Siberia
    c. the Pacific
    d. North America

5. The European power which ruled India was:
    a. France
    b. Britain
    c. Germany
    d. Russia

6. The western power which ruled the Philippines in 1900 was:
    a. France
    b. Britain
    c. Germany
    d. the United States

7. The name of the most famous resistance movement of the West was called:
    a. The Fighters
    b. The Trainers
    c. The Boxers
    d. The Sailors

8. The process of industrialization took Japan _____ years.
    a. 200 years
    b. 150 years
    c. 100 years
    d. less than 100 years

9. The British occupied Egypt in:
    a. 1782
    b. 1822
    c. 1882
    d. 1902

10. The leader of the Sudanese resistance to the West was called:
    a. The Mahdi
    b. The Ulama
    c. The Gadi
    d. The Shah

11. Which African nation remained independent?
    a. Zaire
    b. Zululand
    c. Ethiopia
    d. Egypt

12. The Irish potato famine was caused by:
    a. a fungus
    b. bad weather
    c. insects
    d. poor soil

13. Dreyfus was prosecuted mainly because he was:
    a. a spy
    b. a catholic
    c. a British sympathizer
    d. a Jew

14. Which of the following was pro-imperialist?
    a. Kipling
    b. Conrad
    c. Orwell
    d. Belloc

ESSAY:

1. What was the Dreyfus Affair? Why was it important?

2. What was the Boxer Rebellion? Why did it develop?

3. Where was the burden of imperialism greatest from 1850 –1916? Why?

4. How did Russification differ from other forms of colonialism or imperialism?

5. How did Britain's treatment of Ireland differ from its treatment of India?

CHRONOLOGY:

Match the events listed below to the appropriate place.

```
1750        1775       1800       1825       1850        1875        1900     1925
/_____/_____/_____/_____/_____/_____/_____/
```

A. Young Turks topple Ottoman Sultan
B. Occupation of Egypt
C. Irish potato famine
D. Hati independent
E. Japan wins Russo-Japanese War

MAP EXERCISE:

Label the following cities (refer to map on page 710):
1. Karachi
2. Singapore
3. Hong Kong
4. Bombay
5. Pondicherry
6. Rangoon
7. Saigon
8. Shanghai

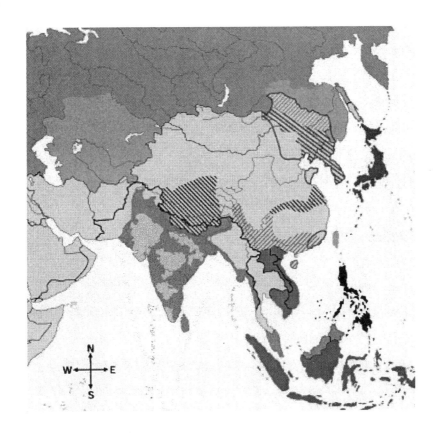

MULTIPLE CHOICE ANSWER KEY:

1. a, p. 706
2. b, p. 706
3. c, p. 706
4. b, p. 709
5. b, p. 712
6. d, p. 714
7. c, p. 718
8. d, p. 719
9. c, p. 721
10. a, p. 723
11. c, p. 725
12. a, p. 727
13. d, p. 728
14. a, p. 731

CHRONOLOGY ANSWER KEY:

Young Turks topple Ottoman Sultan	1908
Occupation of Egypt	1882
Irish potato famine	1845-50
Haiti independent	1804
Japan wins Russo-Japanese War	1905

CHAPTER 24: STORM, STRESS, AND DOUBT
EUROPEAN CULTURE FROM CLASSICISM TO MODERNISM
1780 – 1914

OVERVIEW:

The chapter examines the progeny of the Enlightenment – the development of Western arts and sciences from 1789 until 1914. The progress made during this period was incredible – but this progress itself wrought changes on the meaning of the West.

OUTLINE:

Prologue: Notes from the Underground

I. From Romanticism to Realism
    A. Romanticism and Revolt
    B. Realism and Disenchantment

II. The Sciences and the Schools
    A. The Past as It Really Was
    B. The World as It Came to Be
    C. Sciences of Society
    D. Schooling the Masses

III. Ideals and Ideologies
    A. Liberalism: Freedom and Rights
    B. Conservatism: Valuing Tradition
    C. Nationalism: A Sacred Purpose
    D. Socialism: Sharing the Wealth
    E. Marxism, Communism, Anarchism
    F. Feminism: Rights for Women

IV. *Fin de Siecle* and the Advent of the Modern
    A. New Visions

Conclusion: The Advent of the Modern and the Meaning of the West

IDENTIFICATION:

Classicism

Romanticism

Realism

Sturm und Drang

Goethe

Shelley

Historiography

Historicism

Pasteurization

Spontaneous Generation

Microorganism

Charles Darwin

Social Darwinism

Thomas Malthus

Ideology

Utilitarianism

Class

Proletariat

Syndicalists

Methodists

Pietistic

Modernist

Unconscious

Relativity

Abstract

Atonal

MULTIPLE CHOICE:

1. Romanticism elevates:
    a. logic over structure
    b. feeling over reason
    c. reason over structure
    d. none of the above

2. Realism inspects the world without:
    a. sentiment
    b. color
    c. clarity
    d. none of the above

3. Sturm und Drang means:
    a. light and dark
    b. storm and dark
    c. storm and stress
    d. light and stress

4. The medium best suited to realism is:
    a. music
    b. sculpture
    c. photography
    d. painting

5. Realist literature was generally in the form of:
    a. novels
    b. poems
    c. plays
    d. short stories

6. The first woman to teach at the Sorbonne was:
    a. Durkheim
    b. Dreyfus
    c. Curie
    d. Spencer

7. Liberalism focuses on:
    a. freedom and rights
    b. the value of tradition
    c. love of country
    d. none of the above

8. Socialism focuses on:
    a. freedom and rights
    b. the value of tradition
    c. love of country
    d. sharing of wealth

9. Conservatism focuses on:
    a. freedom and rights
    b. the value of tradition
    c. love of country
    d. sharing of wealth

10. Nihilists promoted attacks on:
    a. church authorities
    b. legal authorities
    c. political authorities
    d. all of the above

11. Parkhurst was a(n):
    a. socialist
    b. feminist
    c. anarchist
    d. none of the above

12. Nietzsche argued that God was:
    a. omnipresent
    b. omnipotent
    c. all-knowing
    d. dead

13. Freud's theories focused on:
    a. the unconscious
    b. the conscious
    c. the unknowable
    d. none of the above

14. Fin de Siecle means end of the:
    a. age
    b. reason
    c. century
    d. time

ESSAY:

1. How did Realism differ from Romanticism? How was it similar?

2. What is Sturm und Drang? Is it uniquely German, or generally Romantic?

3. How was Impressionism different than Realism?

4. Is Nietzsche the logical outgrowth of the Enlightenment's human-central culture? Why or why not?

5. How were the Marxists and the anarchists the same? How were they different?

CHRONOLOGY:

Match the events listed below to the appropriate place.

1750   1775   1800   1825   1850   1875   1900   1925
/_____/_____/_____/_____/_____/_____/_____/

A. Malthus, Essay on Population
B. Communist Manifesto
C. The Interpretation of Dreams
D. Theory of Relativity
E. Origins of Species

MAP EXERCISE:

Locate and label the following major European cultural centers (refer to map on page 739):
1. Berlin
2. Vienna
3. Paris
4. Brussels
5. Amsterdam
6. Copenhagen
7. London
8. Rome
9. Madrid
10. Stockholm
11. St. Petersburg
12. Lisbon
13. Dublin
14. Milan

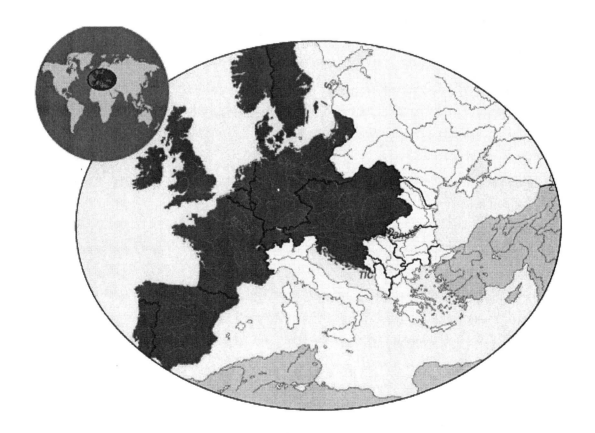

MULTIPLE CHOICE ANSWER KEY:

1. b, p. 740
2. a, p. 740
3. c, p. 742
4. c, p. 743
5. a, p. 743
6. c, p. 748
7. a, p. 752
8. d, p. 755
9. b, p. 753
10. d, p. 758
11. b, p. 759
12. d, p. 760
13. a, p. 762
14. c, p. 760

CHRONOLOGY ANSWER KEY:

Malthus, Essay on Population	1798
Communist Manifesto	1848
The Interpretation of Dreams	1899
Theory of Relativity	1905
Origins of Species	1859

CHAPTER 25: THE MIGHTY ARE FALLEN
THE TRAUMA OF WORLD WAR I
1914 – 1920

OVERVIEW:

At the height of its power, the fundamental changes described previously take root – and lead inexorably to war. As a result, the West loses its total ascendancy over world affairs, and begins to re-conceptualize itself.

OUTLINE:

Prologue: The Generation of 1914

I. Pathways to War
    A. Congresses, Alliances, and Conflicts
    B. Hot Spots
    C. Men and Boys at War

II. In the Midst of Battle
    A. Stalemate in the West
    B. The Eastern Steamroller
    C. At Sea and Abroad
    D. At Home
    E. Russia Turns Back

III. In Search of Peace
    A. Peace Plans
    B. Settlement at Paris
    C. Outcomes

Conclusion: Global War and the Meaning of the West

IDENTIFICATION:

The Crimean War

Pan-Slavism

Junker

U-boats

Edith Cavell

Elam

The Dreadnought

The Lusitania

Duma

Bolshevik

Menshevik

Cadre

Soviet

Rasputin

Lenin

Kerensky

Woodrow Wilson

Reparation

MULTIPLE CHOICE:

1. Pan-Slavism challenged what nation most:
    a. Britain
    b. France
    c. Austria
    d. Belgium

2. Which of the following was a Serbian terrorist organization?
    a. The Junkers
    b. The Black Hand
    c. The Knife
    d. The Luddites

3. Which of the following nations was neutral in 1914?
    a. Hungry
    b. Belgium
    c. Britain
    d. France

4. World War I saw the perfection of what kind of ground warfare?
    a. Trench
    b. Cavalry
    c. Blitzkrieg
    d. none of the above

5. Russia's casualties in World War I were:
    a. 1 million
    b. 2 million
    c. 3 million
    d. 4 million

6. World War I lead to the wide-scale employment of what groups?
    a. Slavs
    b. Women
    c. Jews
    d. Children

7. In 1905, Russia lost a war with:
    a. France
    b. Germany
    c. China
    d. Japan

8. The Treaty of Versailles imposed _____ on Germany.
    a. Democracy
    b. Socialism
    c. reparations
    d. victory

9. True or False: Italy gained territory by the Treaty of Versailles.

10. True or False: Turkey gained territory by the Treaty of Versailles.

11. The United States mobilized how many troops in World War I?
    a. 1 million
    b. 2 million
    c. 3 million
    d. 4 million

12. Wilson's vision of peace had how many points?
    a. 4
    b. 10
    c. 14
    d. 20

13. Lenin was a(n):
    a. Bolshevik
    b. Menshevik
    c. Soldier
    d. Anarchist

14. Trotsky was a(n):
    a. Bolshevik
    b. Menshevik
    c. Anarchist
    d. Czar

ESSAY:

1. Was Pound right that in 1914 the West was a botched civilization? Why?

2. What was the effect of World War I on women's lives?

3. How did the new technology impact World War I?

4. Why was propaganda more important in World War I than in previous conflicts?

5. What ultimately lead to an allied victory in World War I?

CHRONOLOGY:

Match the events listed below to the appropriate place.

```
1860        1870        1880        1890        1900        1910        1920
/_____/_____/_____/_____/_____/_____/____
```

A. Treaty of Versailles
B. Treaty of Brest-Litousk
C. Germany invades Belgium
D. Unification of Italy
E. Slavery abolished in the United States

MAP EXERCISE:

Label the following (refer to map on page 775):
1. Western Front, 1915-1917
2. Furthest Russian advance in west, 1914-1915
3. Maximum extent of advance of Central Powers
4. Balkan Front
5. Jutland 1916
6. Somme
7. Verdun
8. Gallipoli

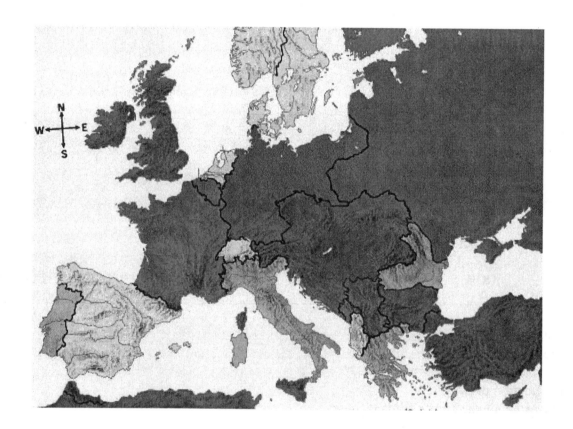

MULTIPLE CHOICE ANSWER KEY:

1. c, p. 771
2. b, p. 773
3. b, p. 775
4. a, p. 779
5. b, p. 783
6. c, p. 748
7. d, p. 789
8. c, p. 795
9. a, p. 797
10. b, p. 797
11. d, p. 784
12. c, p. 792
13. a, p. 789
14. b, p. 789

CHRONOLOGY ANSWER KEY:

Treaty of Versailles	1919
Treaty of Brest-Litousk	1918
Germany invades Belgium	1914
Unification of Italy	1870
Slavery abolished in U.S.	1865

CHAPTER 26: THE TRIUMPH OF UNCERTAINTY CULTURAL INNOVATION, SOCIAL DISRUPTION, AND ECONOMIC COLLAPSE 1915 – 1945

OVERVIEW:

The immediate result of the political collapse described in the previous chapter was a devastating economic collapse – a collapse that gave way to an age of dictators among major western powers.

OUTLINE:

Prologue: The Roll of Dice

I. Uncertainty in the Arts and in Thought
    A. Montage: the Disrupted Narrative
    B. Indeterminacy

II. Uncertain Boundaries: the New Women, the Shrinking Family, the Nurturant State
    A. The New Women
    B. The Shrinking Family and the Nurturant State

III. Economic Uncertainty: From Prosperity to the Breadline
    A. Happy Days
    B. On the Dole

Conclusion: Uncertain Lives and the Meaning of the West

IDENTIFICATION:

Avant-Garde

Cinema

Birth of a Nation

Montage

Marxian Dialectic

Propaganda

Socialist Realism

Jazz Blues

Louie Armstrong

Atom

Logical Positivism

Existentialists

Spiritualism

Fundamentalism

Suffragist

Contraception

Abortion

Margaret Sanger

White Collar

Good Housekeeping

Natalism

Welfare State

Keynesian

New Deal

Franklin Delano Roosevelt

MULTIPLE CHOICE:

1. The terrifying movie of Nazi propaganda was:
    a. The Birth of a Nation
    b. Triumph of the Will
    c. October
    d. none of the above

2. Jazz originated in:
    a. France
    b. North America
    c. Germany
    d. Africa

3. Logical positivism focused on:
    a. feelings
    b. things indisputable
    c. things unknowable
    d. the occult

4. Which of the following flourished in the 1920's?
    a. fundamentalism
    b. spiritualism
    c. Existentialism
    d. all of the above

5. Which of the following first gave women the right to vote?
    a. Norway
    b. Great Britain
    c. France
    d. United States

6. Which of the following last gave women the right to vote?
    a. Norway
    b. Britain
    c. France
    d. United States

7. Garconne means:
    a. girl
    b. boy
    c. girl-boy
    d. none of the above

8. The first official U.S. birth control clinic was founded in the U.S. in _____.
    a. 1882
    b. 1916
    c. 1926
    d. 1932

9. Proponents of nationalism stressed that women should be:
    a. workers
    b. children
    c. mothers
    d. native

10. The Great Crash began in:
    a. 1928
    b. 1929
    c. 1930
    d. 1931

11. World trade decreased in value by what percent from 1929-1932?
    a. 35%
    b. 50%
    c. 60%
    d. 75%

12. Germany in the Jazz Age experienced a currency crisis called:
    a. hyperinflation
    b. depression
    c. stagflation
    d. none of the above

13. The American Plan to end the Depression was called:
    a. The Square Deal
    b. The New Deal
    c. AFL
    d. CIO

14. Keynsian economic theory involved what policy?
    a. cyclical
    b. counter-cyclical
    c. laisez-faire
    d. none of the above

ESSAY:

1. Do you agree with Einstein that a moral world must be based on a rational universe? Why or why not?

2. To what extent did the Jazz Age represent a split between "higher" and "popular" culture? Who decided whether music or art was "high" or "popular"?

3. How was existentialism different than logical positivism? How were both different than fundamentalism?

4. How did the role of women change after World War I? Was the experience in fascist states different?

5. Were economic conditions better in the USA or the USSR in the 1930s? Why?

CHRONOLOGY:

Match the events listed below to the appropriate place.

1900   1910   1920   1930   1940   1950
/_____/_____/_____/_____/_____/_____

A. Hawley-Smoot Turiff
B. Franz Kafka's "The Trial"
C. First birth control clinic opened in New York
D. T.S. Eliot's "The Waste Land"
E. Max Plank's concepts of quantum mechanics

MAP EXERCISE:

Using the map from your text on page 819, label the six nations with the highest debt owed to the United States between the years 1914 to 1925.

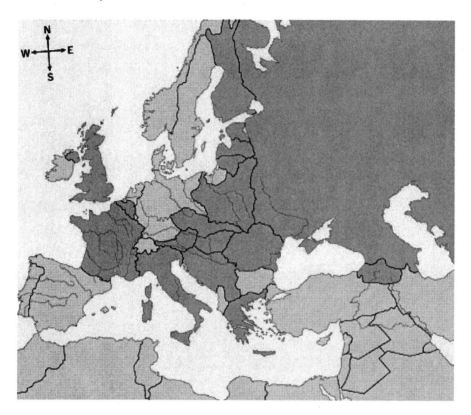

MULTIPLE CHOICE ANSWER KEY:

1. b, p. 804
2. b, p. 806
3. b, p. 809
4. d, p. 810
5. a, p. 811
6. c, p. 811
7. c, p. 812
8. b, p. 814
9. c, p. 818
10. b, p. 820
11. c, p. 820
12. a, p. 822
13. b, p. 828
14. b, p. 827

CHRONOLOGY ANSWER KEY:

Hawley-Smoot Tariff	1930
Franz Kafka's "The Trial"	1925
First birth control clinic opened in New York	1916
T.S. Eliot's "The Waste Land"	1922
Max Plank's concepts of quantum mechanics	1900

CHAPTER 27: STATES IN CONFLICT
COMMUNISM, FASCISM, DEMOCRACY, AND THE CRISIS OF WORLD WAR II 1917 – 1945

OVERVIEW:

The dictators who arose to rule in the aftermath of World War I find themselves at odds. The result is an even more destructive war – one that creates a new world in the shadow of the atomic bomb, and gives birth to the horror of totalitarian regimes.

OUTLINE:

Prologue: The Omnipotent State

I. Bolsheviks and Communists
    A. Lenin: Rewriting Marx
    B. War Communism and the new Economic Policy
    C. Stalin: Gravedigger of the Revolution?
    D. Socialist Realism, Soviet Realities

II. The Faces of Fascism
    A. Fascism
    B. Mussolini and His Imitators
    C. Imperial Japan, Imperialist Ventures
    D. Nazism: the German Form of Fascism

III. The Second World War: Fascism Defeated
    A. The Dictatorships
    B. The Democracies: Frailty and Confusion
    C. The Spanish Civil War: Rehearsal for World War
    D. First Hostilities

IV. Final Solutions

Conclusion: The Defeat of Fascism and the Meaning of the West

IDENTIFICATION:

Totalitarianism

Authoritarian

Fascism

Genocide

Trade Union

Commissariat

Kulaks

Stalin

Gulag

Collectivization

Cosmopolitanism

Corporatist

Fascism

Futurism

Mussolini

Francisco Franco

Nazism

Adolph Hitler

Putsch

Autarky

Volk

Appeasement

Blitzkrieg

Partisans

Holocaust

MULTIPLE CHOICE:

1. Stalin killed what percentage of his officer corps by 1939?
    a. 25%
    b. 50%
    c. 75%
    d. 100%

2. The largest class of people sent to the Gulags were:
    a. Kulaks
    b. Poles
    c. White Russians
    d. Estonians

3. Lenin sought:
    a. worldwide socialism
    b. socialism in one country
    c. agrarianism
    d. none of the above

4. Stalin sought:
    a. worldwide socialism
    b. socialism in one country
    c. agrarianism
    d. none of the above

5. Communism is:
    a. internationalist
    b. nationalistic
    c. ultra-nationalistic
    d. corporatist

6. Fascism is:
    a. corporatist
    b. internationalist
    c. scientific
    d. pacifistic

7. Fascism is:
    a. masculinist
    b. feminist
    c. androgynous
    d. none of the above

8. Mussolini first attacked:
   a. The Vatican
   b. Albania
   c. France
   d. Ethiopia

9. Fascist movements surfaced in which countries:
   a. Britain
   b. France
   c. Greece
   d. all of the above

10. Hitler's death camps killed how many people?
    a. 3 million
    b. 6 million
    c. 9 million
    d. 12 million

11. Hitler's pograms killed how many Jews?
    a. 3 million
    b. 6 million
    c. 9 million
    d. 12 million

12. German war criminals were tried at:
    a. Nuremburg
    b. Versailles
    c. Geneva
    d. The Hague

13. The general who defeated the German tank divisions in Africa was:
    a. Rommel
    b. Montgomery
    c. Patton
    d. Eisenhower

14. The immediate blast of the first atomic bomb killed how many people?
    a. 78,000
    b. 150,000
    c. 300,000
    d. 178,000

ESSAY:

1. Why did the Kulaks initially support the Bolsheviks? Why were they later targeted?

2. Who was more evil – Stalin or Hitler? Why?

3. What are the elements of fascism? How do they compare with communism?

4. What were the causes of the Holocaust? How many died as a result?

5. Why did Hitler attack the Soviet Union? If he had not done so, do you think Stalin would have attacked him? Why?

CHRONOLOGY:

Match the events listed below to the appropriate place.

1910   1920   1930   1940   1950
/_____/_____/_____/_____/___

A. Trotsky murdered
B. Nuremburg Trials
C. Japan Surrenders
D. VE Day
E. Treaty of Versailles

MAP EXERCISE:

Label the following concentration camp sites (refer to map on page 861):
1. Treblinka
2. Auschwitz-Birkenau
3. Dachau
4. Buchenwald
5. Bergen-Belsen
6. Stutthof

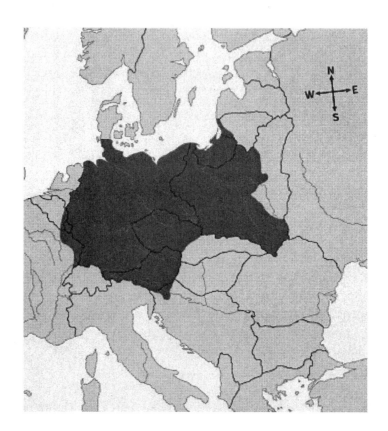

MULTIPLE CHOICE ANSWER KEY:

1. b, p. 837
2. a, p. 837
3. a, p. 835
4. b, p. 837
5. a, p. 842
6. a, p. 842
7. a, p. 842
8. d, p. 844
9. d, p. 845
10. c, p. 863
11. b, p. 863
12. a, p. 863
13. b, p. 858
14. a, p. 866

CHRONOLOGY ANSWER KEY:

Trotsky murdered	1940
Nuremburg Trials	November 20, 1945
Japan Surrenders	August 14, 1945
VE Day	May 8, 1945
Treaty of Versailles	1919

CHAPTER 28: THE END OF IMPERIALISM
DECOLONIZATION AND STATEBUILDING AROUND THE GLOBE
1914 – 1990s

OVERVIEW:

Impelled by the destruction of two world wars, the West officially gives up it political dominance over most of the world. The exception is the United States, whose economic power allows it to remain dominant in an era of decolonization.

OUTLINE:

Prologue: Sunset and Sunrise

I. Fading Empires: Anti-Colonialism and Decolonization
    A. The Sun Sets on the British Empire
    B. Reluctant Disengagement

II. New World Orders: Statebuilding in Africa, the Middle East, and Asia
    A. Statebuilding in Africa
    B. Statebuilding in the Middle East
    C. Statebuilding in Asia

III. The Last Imperialist: The United States Abroad and At Home
    A. Good Neighbors
    B. The Domino Game
    C. The Color Line: Conflict at Home

Conclusion: The Shadows of Imperialism and the Meaning of the West

IDENTIFICATION:

Decolonization

Dominions

Commonwealth

Mandates

Colonialism

Animist

Apartheid

Young Turks

Islamist

Shi'ite

Mao Zedong

Reeducation

Manifest destiny

Counter-insurgency

The Cold War

Vietnamization

Reservations

Harlem Renaissance

Marcus Garvey

Anti-colonialism

MULTIPLE CHOICE:

1. Mahatma Gahndi was killed by a(n) _____ extremist.
    a. British
    b. Japanese
    c. Muslim
    d. Hindu

2. Britain released sovereignty over Ireland completely in:
    a. 1916
    b. 1927
    c. 1937
    d. 1969

3. France released sovereignty over Algeria in:
    a. 1952
    b. 1962
    c. 1969
    d. 1979

4. Apartheid means:
    a. separateness
    b. segregation
    c. slavery
    d. communist

5. Ulamma is based on _____ -centered rule.
    a. state
    b. city
    c. village
    d. family

6. The movement to unseat the Ottoman Sultan was conducted by the ____ Turks.
    a. Old
    b. Communist
    c. Young
    d. Fascist

7. Which Egyptian leader made peace with Israel:
    a. Nasser
    b. Sadat
    c. Kemal
    d. Hussein

8. Which Egyptian seized the Suez Canal?
    a. Nasser
    b. Sadat
    c. Kemal
    d. Hussein

9. Intellectuals during the Cultural Revolution were sent to camps for:
    a. reeducation
    b. extermination
    c. harmonization
    d. none of the above

10. The last imperialist nation is:
    a. the United States
    b. Germany
    c. France
    d. the Soviet Union

11. How many Americans died in the Vietnam War?
    a. 28,000
    b. 58,000
    c. 128,000
    d. 158,000

12. W.E.B. Du Bois died in:
    a. Georgia
    b. France
    c. Ghana
    d. California

13. Castro took over power from what leader?
    a. Kennedy
    b. Batisa
    c. Juarez
    d. Diaz

14. The United States invaded Vera Cruz in?
    a. 1900
    b. 1914
    c. 1924
    d. 1934

ESSAY:

1. What was the immediate effect of Britain leaving India? What were some of the long-term impacts?

2. What was the immediate effect of France's decision not to leave Vietnam? What were some of the long-term impacts?

3. Did the massive decolonization by the West signal waning influence? If not, why not?

4. How do the imperial policies of the United States differ from earlier imperialist models? How are they similar?

5. Why did caudillism hang on so long in Latin America?

CHRONOLOGY:

Match the events listed below to the appropriate place.

```
1880       1900       1920       1940       1960       1980       2000
/_____/_____/_____/_____/_____/_____/_____
```

A. Suez Canal Nationalized
B. Gulf War
C. Partition of India
D. Mandela elected President
E. French leave Indochina

MAP EXERCISE:

Label the 1939 colonial possessions of the following countries (refer to map on page 871):
1. Great Britain
2. France
3. Spain
4. Portugal
5. Belgium
6. Italy

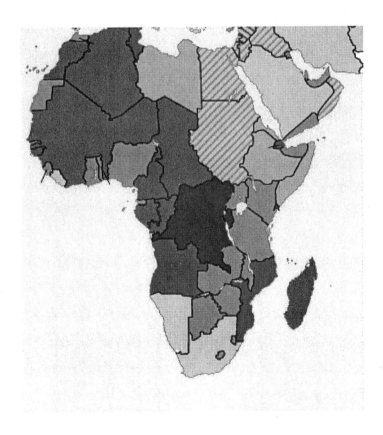

MULTIPLE CHOICE ANSWER KEY:

1. d, p. 873
2. c, p. 874
3. b, p. 875
4. a, p. 879
5. c, p. 881
6. c, p. 881
7. b, p. 882
8. a, p. 882
9. b, p. 887
10. a, p. 890
11. b, p. 899
12. c, p. 900
13. b, p. 894
14. b, p. 891

CHRONOLOGY ANSWER KEY:

Suez Canal Nationalized	1956
Gulf War	1991
Partition of India	1947
Mandela elected President	1994
French leave Indochina	1954

CHAPTER 29: BACK FROM ARMAGEDDON
FROM THE BOMB TO THE INTERNET
1945 – 1990

OVERVIEW:

The United States and the Soviet Union – the last two Western powers with global capacities – struggle mightily against one another. Ultimately, the United States wins and imposes its view of culture and economy on the world systems – even as the West itself begins to question the means by which it has triumphed.

OUTLINE:

Prologue: Reprieve from MAD: 1989

I. Apocalypse Now?
    A. Postwar Polarization
    B. Cold War Confrontations
    C. The Cold War on the Global Stage
    D. Armageddon Deferred: 1985 – 1991

II. All You Need is Love
    A. Rolling Stones
    B. Women of Worth
    C. Love Your Mother
    D. Last Battles

Conclusion: Retreat from Armageddon and the Meaning of the West

IDENTIFICATION:

Velvet Revolution

Repatriation

"The Big Three"

The Berlin Airlift

Cybernetics

The Truman Doctrine

De-Stalinization

Detente

Glasnost

Perestroika

"Rock 'n' roll"

"Hard rock"

Maternalist

Suttee

Female circumcision

Diaspora

Silent Spring

Genocide

MULTIPLE CHOICE:

1. The Post World War II plan to rebuild Europe was the _____ Plan.
    a. Tito
    b. Stalin
    c. Marshal
    d. Repatriation

2. The Truman Doctrine announced the strategy of:
    a. containment
    b. appeasement
    c. roll-back
    d. Vietnamization

3. The country to launch the first satellite was:
    a. the USA
    b. the USSR
    c. Germany
    d. Great Britain

4. The first civilians executed in the U.S. for espionage were the:
    a. Rosenbergs
    b. McCarthys
    c. Stanleys
    d. Seegers

5. In 1956, Soviet forces invaded:
    a. Czechoslovakia
    b. Hungary
    c. Austria
    d. Afghanistan

6. In 1968, Soviet forces invaded:
    a. Czechoslovakia
    b. Hungary
    c. Austria
    d. Afghanistan

7. In what year did the Soviet Union finally disintegrate?
    a. 1989
    b. 1990
    c. 1991
    d. 1992

8. Which of the following has the smallest gender gap?
    a. Canada
    b. Ireland
    c. Australia
    d. India

9. Which of the following has the least % number of literate women?
    a. Cuba
    b. Afghanistan
    c. China
    d. Vietnam

10. The Earth's population in 1996 was:
    a. 2.5 billion
    b. 5.8 billion
    c. 1.625 billion
    d. 8.25 billion

11. Which has the largest population growth in 1993?
    a. USA
    b. China
    c. Angola
    d. Brazil

12. What fraction of Cambodians were killed by the Khmer Rouge?
    a. 1/2
    b. 1/5
    c. 1/7
    d. 1/10

13. Which of the following generally does not have a policy of extra-judicial killing?
    a. Morocco
    b. Algeria
    c. Columbia
    d. Indonesia

14. Which of the following did not disintegrate after 1990?
    a. Yugoslavia
    b. Czechoslovakia
    c. Rwanda
    d. South Africa

ESSAY:

1. Why did the capitalist powers win the Cold War? Was that victory inevitable, or was it ever in doubt?

2. To what extent was Western Culture after World War II shaped by the threat of atomic warfare?

3. What was detente? Was it significant?

4. To what extent was music in the 1960s a unifying force? To what extent did it spawn disunity?

5. To what extend did the women's movement after World War II reject its earlier positions? To what extent was it a continuation of earlier struggles?

CHRONOLOGY:

Match the events listed below to the appropriate place.

```
1940      1950      1960      1970      1980      1990      2000
/_____/_____/_____/_____/_____/_____/_____
```

A. Cuban Missile Crisis
B. Dayton Peace Agreement
C. Collapse of Communism
D. NATO formed
E. Woodstock Music Festival

MAP EXERCISE:

Using the map on page 909 of your text, label six nations that were major Cold War flashpoints:

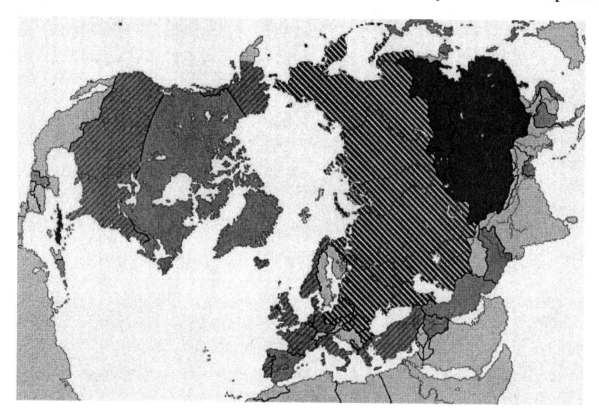

MULTIPLE CHOICE ANSWER KEY:

1. c, p. 910
2. a, p. 911
3. b, p. 913
4. a, p. 914
5. a, p. 916
6. b, p. 916
7. c, p. 921
8. a, p. 930
9. b, p. 931
10. b, p. 933
11. c, p. 934
12. c, p. 941
13. a, p. 942
14. d, p. 941

CHRONOLOGY ANSWER KEY:

Cuban Missile Crisis	1961
Dayton Peace Agreement	1995
Collapse of Communism	1989
NATO formed	1949
Woodstock Music Festival	1969

CHAPTER 30: EPILOGUE
THE LAST DECADE: WHERE WE'VE BEEN AND WHAT MAY BE
The 1990s

OVERVIEW:

The dominance of the United States has not ended global problems – but the United States, and the rest of the West seem to be the first culture to consciously struggle against the history and domination. Only time will tell whether this struggle will be won, or horrendously lost.

OUTLINE:

Prologue: The Westward Journey

I. Reconciliation

II. Unification

III. Globalization

IV. The End of the West?

Conclusion: The Past, The Future, and the Meaning of the West

IDENTIFICATION:

"The Short Century"

Christian Democratic

NATO

The Common Market

Hegemony

Globalization

The Euro

Heroization

"New Age"

"The West"

MULTIPLE CHOICE:

1. Increasing economic interconnectedness is called:
    a. Democracy
    b. Cosmopolitanism
    c. Globalization
    d. Regionalism

2. Fukuyama argued that the world has reached the end of:
    a. History
    b. Democracy
    c. Liberalism
    d. Currency

3. The unified currency of Europe is the:
    a. Pound
    b. Mark
    c. Euro
    d. Dollar

4. Which European country did not have a G.N.P. over $10,000 per capita in 1991:
    a. Portugal
    b. Spain
    c. Ireland
    d. Iceland

5. According to Bernard Lewis, the unique aspect of the West is its:
    a. desire to conquer
    b. enslavement
    c. discovery
    d. repentance

6. According to Landes, the biggest struggle in the next century will be between:
    a. East and West
    b. North and South
    c. Tradition and Progress
    d. Rich and Poor

7. The two main poles of European culture today are:
    a. Paris and Bonn
    b. London and Bonn
    c. Paris and London
    d. Rome and Bonn

8. Huntington believes that the West will:
    a. decline
    b. ascend
    c. conquer
    d. none of the above

9. Which of the following was communist state in 1999?
    a. Russian
    b. France
    c. Cuba
    d. Nicaragua

10. Britain has ruled that political leaders are not immune from prosecution for:
    a. violations of treaties
    b. violations of Human Rights
    c. declarations of War
    d. none of the above

ESSAY:

1. Do you agree with Havel's assessment that we are headed for a global society? Why or why not?

2. Is the West in decline? Can that decline be stopped? If it could be stopped, should it?

3. What is postmodernism? How does it impact western culture?

4. Why do people claim that the 20th century was short? Was it?

5. What are the core values of the West?

MAP EXERCISE:

Using the map on page 951, label the nations that were part of the second wave of applicant EU members:

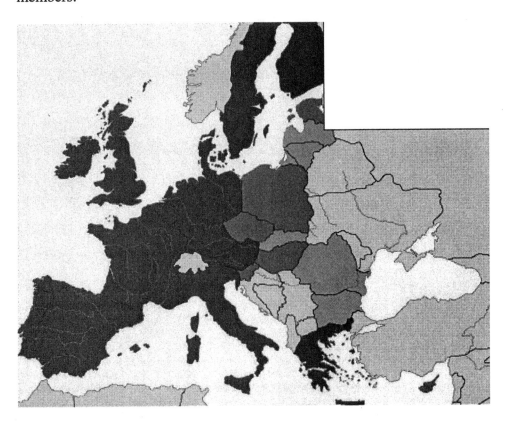

MULTIPLE CHOICE ANSWER KEY:

1. c, p. 951
2. a, p. 951
3. c, p. 952
4. a, p. 953
5. d, p. 954
6. d, p. 958
7. b, p. 952
8. a, p. 955
9. c, p. 948
10. b, p. 948